Wired

Sigmund Brouwer

Orca currents

ORCA BOOK PUBLISHERS

National Library of Canada Cataloguing in Publication Data

Brouwer, Sigmund, 1959-
Wired / Sigmund Brouwer.

(Orca currents)
ISBN 978-1-55143-478-0

I. Title. II. Series.

PS8553.R68467W57 2005   JC813'.54   C2005-904404-7

First published in the United States, 2005
Library of Congress Control Number: 2005929719

Summary: Keegan must snowboard to safety.

Orca Book Publishers gratefully acknowledges the support for its publishing
programs provided by the following agencies: the Government of Canada
through the Canada Book Fund and the Canada Council for the Arts,
and the Province of British Columbia through the BC Arts Council
and the Book Publishing Tax Credit.

Cover design by Lynn O'Rourke
Cover photography by First Light

ORCA BOOK PUBLISHERS   ORCA BOOK PUBLISHERS
PO Box 5626, Stn. B   PO Box 468
Victoria, BC Canada   Custer, WA USA
V8R 6S4   98240-0468

www.orcabook.com
Printed and bound in Canada.
Printed on 100% PCW recycled paper.

13 12 11 10 • 7 6 5 4

chapter one

I stood at the top of the mountain. Above me was bright blue sky and pale winter sun. Below me was a mile to the finish line. Steve, my coach, stood beside me. He wanted me to reach the finish line in less time than it takes to eat a sandwich.

"Keegan," he said. "I see that look on your face."

"What look?"

"You're thinking about Garth. Don't."

Yes, I was thinking about Garth, one of the other racers on the team. Garth had broken both his legs during a time trial a couple of weeks earlier. And just like the run that had hurt him, this was a time trial too. I had to ace this run if I wanted to keep my number-one spot on the racing team. But that meant going really fast. And fast meant I could get hurt like Garth.

"Quit worrying about the speed, Keegan. Relax."

When someone tells you not to think about something, it is the first thing you think of.

Speed. When I reached full speed my skis would be moving at 110 kilometers an hour. I would be standing on those skis. This meant I, too, would be moving 110 kilometers an hour. That is almost as fast as people fall from airplanes. Before they open their parachute.

I didn't have a parachute. Worse, skis are about as wide as a credit card and not much thicker. As a downhill skier, my job is to stand on those thin flat pieces of plastic and metal and make sure I don't fall.

What I really don't like to think about is that 110 kilometers an hour is the same as traveling thirty meters a second. My friend Mike, who likes to scare me, figured that out. Worse, after figuring it out he told me. So now I know that in the time it takes for me to breathe in and out my body will shoot the length of a football field.

At that speed, if I fall off those thin flat pieces of plastic and metal I will spend the rest of my life in a hospital. Eating jelly. Drinking warm milk. Getting yelled at by big ugly nurses.

"Keegan, I still see that look on your face."

"Sorry," I said. I smiled, hiding what I always hide on the slopes. I am a coward.

"That's better," he told me. "Are you ready?"

"Sure," I lied like I always did. I wasn't going to let anyone know I was afraid. Not Keegan Bishop, provincial champion downhill skier. No one was supposed to know my biggest secret.

"Now remember, when you get to the bottom confirm with the timekeeper that you're our last guy today. We'll be opening the run for the public as soon as you're down the hill."

I nodded.

Steve continued. "And remind the officials that your number is wrong."

On my back was a small jersey with big white numbers. Another guy on the team, Budgie McGee, had accidently taken my number. We hadn't noticed until he had gone, so I had his number on my back. It didn't matter, though, as long as I told the guys with the clipboards at the bottom of the hill.

I looked over at the timekeeper at the top. He nodded.

"Go!" My coach yelled.

I went.

I blinked twice. The wind filled my lungs. It filled my ears like the roar of a freight train.

I cut left to miss a boulder sticking out of the snow. I ducked beneath a branch. I hit a jump at freeway speed. It launched me into the air at least one story off the ground. I leaned forward and made sure my skis stayed straight.

I thumped back to earth and crouched low, so I would block less wind. At this speed, the trees on each side of the slope seemed like flashing fence boards.

Halfway down the run I knew I was skiing the best I ever had. If I kept pushing, I would easily stay at number one.

Beneath my helmet, I grinned my grin of fear. And as I cut into a steep turn, I saw it. But couldn't believe it.

Wire. Black wire stretched between two trees at waist height. I was flashing toward it at thirty meters per second. Hitting the wire at that speed would slice me in two.

chapter two

I dropped my poles and crouched lower on my skis. At 110 kilometers per hour this was not as easy as sitting down for supper. But I had no choice.

The wire scraped the top of my helmet as I slid beneath it. I wobbled. To keep my balance, I slapped my hand on the snow. My hand bounced off. I nearly fell over the other way. I fought to stay on my skis for another hundred meters. The sky tilted around me.

The snow seemed to spin. The trees were rising and falling at crazy angles. Still I did not fall.

Finally, I was able to turn and dig the edges of my skis into the snow. I began to slow down.

Just when I thought I was safe, I hit a patch of ice. My skis slid out from under me. I began to tumble and roll down the hill. I felt like a cannon ball rolling down a set of stairs.

The best thing to do in a fall is also the hardest thing to do. You have to make yourself go limp like a rag doll. If you are too tense, you can rip your muscles and snap your bones.

I waited to stop tumbling. It wasn't until I fell into some deep soft snow at the edge of the trees that I finally stopped.

I tasted for blood. Sometimes when you fall you bite your tongue. No blood.

I blinked. My eyelids worked. I wiggled my fingers. They worked too. So did my arms. And my legs. That was a good sign. If I could move all my body parts, then I hadn't broken my back.

This made me want to quit. Again. Every time I fell, I wanted to quit. Every time I stood at the top, waiting to begin another run, I wanted to quit. That's what fear will do to a person. But I couldn't let anyone know I was afraid.

But this had been too close. I could have ended up like Garth who was still in a hospital. Eating jelly. Drinking warm milk. Getting yelled at by big ugly nurses.

I took off my helmet and shook my hair loose.

Then I realized something. Black wire stretched between two trees is not an accident. What if something similar had happened to Garth?

If Garth's broken legs hadn't been an accident, there were questions I didn't want to think about.

Like who was doing this? And why?

I had my questions. But I also had something else to worry about.

The wire was still stretched between the trees. This run was closed for the racers to use for time trials. I had been the last one in our group to go. That meant I didn't have to worry about anyone else on our team. But now that I was finished, the run would be open to other skiers.

Any minute, someone else might come over the hill—someone who wouldn't be able to duck in time. A wire like that could kill a person.

I stepped on the bindings and popped my boots loose from the skis. I tried to stay on the hard-packed run, but running back up the hill wasn't easy. My boots kept sinking into the snow. I felt like I was in one of those dreams where the monster is chasing you and your shoes seem to be glued to the ground.

I kept looking up the hill for skiers. I was ready to yell a warning if I saw someone.

I made it to the wire. No skiers yet. My heart was ready to explode. Running uphill in snow and ski boots is hard work.

I saw that the end of the wire was wrapped around one tree and twisted tight. It would have been easier if I had pliers. But all I had were fingers and fear.

I began to untwist. The wire was heavy and stiff. It cut through my ski gloves. I kept untwisting. It cut into the skin of my fingers. Finally, I had it nearly unwrapped.

I heard the sound of skis on snow. Someone was coming down the hill!

All I saw was the shiny purple of a ski suit and flying blonde hair as the girl came over the top of the rise. She was headed straight toward the wire. Not on skis, but on a snowboard.

"Stop!" I shouted. "Stop!"

I was too late.

She was going fast and didn't have a chance. The wire caught her across the middle of her body.

She screamed.

I thought the wire would slice her to pieces. It didn't. She hit the wire hard and yanked loose the last bit of wire that was still around the tree. She flipped over. As she fell, her snowboard and ankles got caught in the wire. She slid until she reached the end of the wire and then she snapped to a stop like a dog running to the end of its leash.

The girl yelped.

I ran over as fast as I could. "Are you all right?" I asked as I helped her to her feet.

She didn't thank me for saving her life. She punched me in the face.

chapter three

"Hey!" I shouted. "What was that for?"

"You jerk!" she shouted back. "You could have killed me!"

She took another swing at me. I grabbed her wrist just before her fist hit my face a second time.

"Killed you?" I was breathing hard from running. My face hurt from her punch. And now this girl in a purple ski suit thought I had tried to kill her? "No way, I was trying to—"

"Do you think that kind of joke is funny?" She pulled her arm away from me. She gave me a dirty look. "What if you had tied the wire completely tight before I hit it? It could have sliced me in two."

"I was trying to untie it."

"Sure," she said. It didn't sound like she believed me.

She reached into her jacket and pulled out a cell phone.

"Could we talk about this before you call the police or anyone else?" I said, "Here, look at my fingers. See the blood? I was trying to untie the wire when you came down."

"Or," she said, "you were just finished tying it and couldn't get away in time."

"Sure. I'm on a timed run for the racing team and thought I'd just stop for a few minutes. You know, because I'm so much faster than anyone I wanted to give them a chance."

She snapped her cell phone shut.

"So maybe you're telling the truth about the wire," she said.

"Maybe?" I pointed at my skis farther down the hill.

"See," I said. "The wire nearly got me too. That's where I fell. I came back up the hill in case anyone was behind me."

She stared at me for long seconds.

"I'm sorry," she said. She looked at the ground. "You probably saved my life."

In a movie, she would have leaned forward and kissed me.

This wasn't a movie. I licked blood off my lip. It was dripping from my nose where she had punched me. Instead of kissing me, she unzipped a pocket and found some tissue. She wiped the blood off my face.

"What's your name?" she asked. She had an accent and spoke like the tourists from New York. Her hair was blonde and straight. She had light green eyes. She looked like she could be a model.

"Keegan Bishop." I waited for her to say something about me being a great skier. Everyone who skied here had heard of me.

"Keegan," she said. "I like that name. Are you a racer?"

I grinned. "You've heard of me?"

"No. I see the racing number on your back. And you just told me you were on a timed run."

How dumb did I feel? I tried to change the subject. "Are you from around here? Or are you on Christmas vacation?"

"My name's Cassie," she told me. "Cassie Holt. Thanks for asking."

Again I felt dumb. She probably thought I didn't care enough to know her name.

A couple of skiers appeared. They didn't say anything and just skied past.

I wondered when one of the ski officials would show up to see why I hadn't made it to the bottom yet. I was going to wait right here. I wanted them to see why I had fallen. That way, I would get another chance to run my time trial.

It seemed like Cassie and I had gone a long time without talking.

"Well," Cassie finally said. "If you didn't put the wire there, who did?"

"I'd like to know. Just so that I could strangle them."

She smiled. "You're too cute to be that mean."

I didn't know what to say to that.

Cassie stepped out of her snowboard. She carried it under her arm and started to climb back up the hill. I stood there staring at her purple ski suit and the blonde hair that hung down her back.

"Come on," she said.

"Where?"

"To the other tree."

"We'll just pull the wire out of the way," I said. My hands hurt badly. The cold did not help either. "We don't need to untie the other side too."

Besides, I needed the wire around the tree so my coach and the timekeepers would believe my story.

"Who said anything about untying it?" she asked.

She walked all the way up to the other tree. She propped her snowboard in the snow and looked at the base of the tree without moving. I finally walked up and stood beside her.

"Look at that," she said, pointing at marks in the snow.

"What?"

"Tracks. Whoever tied the wire to this tree stood right there."

"Maybe we should get a bloodhound," I said.

"Very funny, Keegan Bishop. Notice anything about that track?"

"Belongs to a snowboard," I told her. It was a single, wide track. From the marks in the snow, I could see where someone had walked around the tree and tied the wire. I could see that the person had stepped onto a snowboard and gone down a trail through the trees. There was no way of finding the person now.

"Snowboard," Cassie repeated. "So already you know something about the person who did this."

"That doesn't help much," I said. "There's only about a thousand people who snowboard on this hill. Of course, not all of them are as good as this person. Whoever it was chose a tough trail to get away."

"Probably didn't want to be seen."

"And if the person wasn't seen, there's no chance of proving who did this."

"Not quite," she said. She pointed at a branch a little higher than my head. I saw some blue fuzz stuck to the end of the branch. "The snowboarder who did this wears a blue knitted hat—one that rubbed against that branch. Which means we are looking for someone as tall as you."

She put her hands on her hips and grinned at me. "A snowboarder who wears a blue hat, is tall and good on a snowboard. There, now you know four things about the person who did this."

She paused and pulled out her cell phone again.

"You have a cell phone?" she asked.

I nodded. My parents didn't have a lot of money. But that was one thing they were willing to buy me. In case I ever had an accident, or needed them in an emergency or if they worried about me and just wanted to call.

"What's your number?" she asked.

I gave it to her. "In case you need someone to hang with on the slopes?" I asked.

"In case I find any information you might find helpful. I'll send you a text message."

"Oh," I said. I grinned. "What are you? A detective?"

Her grin turned into a frown. "I've got to go now."

"What did I say?" I asked.

She grabbed her snowboard.

"Cassie?" I tried again. "What did I say wrong?"

She didn't answer. She left without looking back.

This girl had punched me in the face. She had wiped blood from my nose. She had insulted me. And she had left without saying goodbye.

This was some kind of girl. I hoped I would meet her again soon.

chapter four

In the winter, I put knobby tires on my mountain bike. What I do, when the weather isn't bad, is take it up to the ski hill with me. Well, not with me—with the person who gives me a ride. Most of the older skiers on the team drive. With the bike at the top of the hill, I've got a way to get home at the end of my training, and I don't have to wait for anyone else. Usually, the roads are cleared of snow, and when they are not, I leave the bike at the top of the hill and catch a ride with someone.

I didn't ride my bike straight home after finishing the day on the slopes.

I wanted to, but I knew I had to force myself to go to the one place in town that brought back the worst memories of my life.

That would be the hospital.

From the ski hill, there were two ways to get to the hospital: the short way and the long way.

I couldn't take the long way because I didn't want to be late for supper. That meant I had to take the short way. I had to take the one road in to town that I always did my best to avoid—the road with a railway crossing. The crossing that now has warning lights and cross bars that come down when a train is coming. When I was a kid, there were no warning lights.

I came to a stop at the tracks.

Someone behind me honked, angry that I had stopped for no reason.

Maybe it was no reason to them, but I couldn't help myself.

I looked both ways to make sure that a locomotive wasn't bearing down on the crossing, horn blaring, huge bright headlight like the eye of a monster.

No train. Only the memory of something terrible, bearing down on me with the same force as a locomotive, a memory I couldn't escape.

I gritted my teeth and rode my bike across the tracks.

Ahead was the hospital.

Garth was in a room by himself in a big bed. His legs were in casts up to his waist. He wore a pajama top. There was a bowl of Jell-O on a tray in front of him. He didn't look happy.

"Keegan," he said. "This is a surprise."

It probably was. Garth Norwood was not exactly my friend. He was a little bigger than I was, and he was the kind of guy who tried to push other people around. Right after I had joined the ski team, I'd heard him yelling at one of the younger skiers. When I'd told him to stop being a bully, he'd thrown a punch. Which I ducked. Then I'd thrown him to the ground and told him if he did something like that again, I would punch back. He hadn't tried anything since.

"How are you?" he asked. He had long blond hair and a moustache.

"Almost not good," I said. "That's why I'm here. I nearly ended up in the hospital too."

"Really? During time trials?"

"Yes." I told Garth what had happened with the wire.

"Wow!" he said. "That sounds terrible."

"What happened to you?" I asked. "All we've heard is that the coach found you knocked out in the snow. With your legs broken. Do you think maybe you could have hit a wire or something?"

"Nope," he said. "I crossed my skis. It's a stupid thing to do at the speed of a rocket."

"That's true," I said. "Very stupid."

"How's everyone else on the team? Did anything happen to anyone else?"

"No," I said. "Except for a mix-up in jerseys, nothing else happened."

I told Garth how Budgie McGee had accidently switched numbers with me before the time trials.

We both laughed at that. Budgie was Garth's best friend. Everyone called him Budgie because his name was Bud G. McGee, and he had a tiny nose that made him look like a budgie bird.

After laughing about Budgie, Garth and I couldn't find much more to talk about. It was like when we traveled on the bus to ski races. Garth and I didn't like being around each other.

"Well," I finally said. "Time to go. I've got to get my homework done."

"Sure," he said.

I stood up. I got halfway to the door.

"Keegan."

I looked back at him.

"Yes, Garth?"

"Could you take this stupid meal tray?" he asked. "Maybe set it on that table over there by the door?"

I walked back to his bed. He took his tray and leaned forward to give it to me. For a moment, his pajama top fell open. I was looking down at the tray, so I saw his chest and stomach. I didn't say anything about it, though. I set the tray on a table and said goodbye again.

As I walked down the long hallway, I thought about Garth's stomach. I didn't like what I was thinking.

When his pajama top fell open, I saw that his entire stomach was black and blue. It looked like a giant bruise. It looked like the kind of bruise a wire cable would make if a skier hit it at full speed.

If Garth had hit a cable stretched between two trees, why had he lied to me and everybody else about it?

Mom's back was to me as I walked into the kitchen for supper. I could see from the side that she was stirring meat sauce into a bowl of spaghetti noodles.

Dad was at the kitchen table, staring at the clock on the wall. All the place settings were ready for us to eat. I'd barely made it on time. Whenever I was late, my parents panicked. It hurt them most when I was late for supper though, because it reminded them of something that was always hiding beneath the surface of their lives.

Mom and Dad had been married for nearly twenty years. Their grad photos showed them bright and smiling, but now they mainly looked tired.

Dad looked from the clock to me. He shook his head and frowned when he noticed I was limping. He put a finger to his lip, silently telling me not to say a word about it. Like I needed that reminder.

"Hi, Keegan," Mom said, putting the spaghetti bowl in the center of the table. "How did everything go today on the ski hill?"

I sat down. I knew the answer she wanted. And I knew the answer Dad always wanted me to give.

"Great," I said.

"No falls?" she asked.

"None," I said. My leg was beginning to hurt, but I would force myself not to limp when I left the table, in case she was watching. "You know me," I said. "I never push too hard."

"That's my boy." She leaned over and kissed my forehead. "You know how I worry."

I did not feel bad about lying to her. She wanted me to lie. She wanted to believe my lies. Really. She always seemed so breakable, and I think that's how she dealt with life.

"Well," Dad said, "Didn't your mom make another great meal today?"

"She sure did," I said. Mom patted my hand. I patted her hand back.

Yes. We were the perfect family in the perfect household. The laundry was always clean and folded. The floors were always vacuumed. The dishes were always done as soon as we were finished eating. No one yelled at anyone, ever. We only watched PG movies.

We were the perfect household.

So what if it had taken me years of begging and fighting with my parents for permission to ski? So what if the only reason my dad allowed me to ski was that I had promised never to tell Mom about anything dangerous that happened during my runs?

Yes. We were perfect. Except for one thing. There should have been a fourth person eating with us.

chapter five

The next morning I took the chairlift to the top of the mountain. The sun was out again. The sky was bright bluc, so pretty it almost hurt my eyes. There was no wind. And it was warmer than usual. It was a perfect day to ski.

But I wasn't thinking about skiing.

As the chair moved up the mountain, I hardly noticed the skiers and snowboarders going down the hill below me. All I could think about was the cable wire between the trees.

Somebody had tried to hurt me.

I needed to find out who and why. If I didn't, that somebody might try again. The next time, though, I might not be so lucky. I was fifteen. I wanted to make it to my sixteenth birthday. And then to many more until I was an old man. Running into cable wire at high speeds would not help my chances.

I needed to be a detective, only I knew a lot more about racing on skis than I did about looking for bad guys.

I grinned into the sunshine, thinking about something else. All of this would be more fun if Cassie Holt was helping me.

What had she said to me? The person who did this was a tall person with a blue hat who could snowboard really well.

That meant the first place I should look was where the snowboarders hung out. Which was where I was going. All the good snow-boarders liked a run called the Pipeline.

When I got off the chairlift, I skied over to that hill.

From the top, the run did look like a huge pipe with the top half cut off. Both sides of the run curved downward into the middle. I thought of the curved walls that skateboarders use to do their tricks. There were trees on either side of the run.

I took my skis off and stuck them into the snow. I watched the snowboarders. They did look like skateboarders as they went up and down the walls of the pipeline. They did flips and turns. They did jumps and wipeouts.

I heard the crunch of snow. I turned my head and looked upward. For a second, I couldn't see who had moved beside me. The sun was too bright.

"Hello, Keegan Bishop."

The voice belonged to Cassie Holt.

"Hello," I said.

"Thinking of becoming a boardhead?" she asked.

"Bored?" I asked. "No, actually I find this interesting. It looks a lot different than skiing."

She laughed. "I didn't ask if you found this boring. A boardhead is someone who snowboards."

"I knew that," I said. "I was just testing you."

"Right." She gave me a smile. "I've been asking people about you."

"Really?" My heart started beating faster. Did this mean she had been thinking about me like I had been thinking about her?

"Really. They tell me that you live to be a downhill racer. So I can understand that you don't know much about snowboarding."

"Well," I said. "I'm training as hard as I can to be a pro. It takes most of my time."

There was plenty I didn't tell her. Like the real reason I forced myself to do something I was so afraid of, or that after most ski races I went to the bathroom and threw up.

She smiled. "So why are you wasting time here?"

"I'm looking for a tall snowboarder with a blue hat," I told her. "Remember? Because of your..."

I stopped myself. If I said detective work, would she get mad again?

"Because of my detective work?" she asked. "Don't worry. I won't leave. Yesterday I had a reason. Today I don't."

"What's the reason?"

"I can't tell you," she said. "Will you trust me on that?"

"Sure," I said.

Someone shouted at us.

"Hey, Cassie!" It was a guy on a snowboard, coming down from the top of the hill. The sun was in my eyes so I couldn't see his face.

He stopped fast. He used the edge of his snowboard to throw snow all over me.

I stood up. The guy was a little taller than me. Though I didn't know his name, I had seen him before. He was one of the regular snowboarders. "That's a jerk thing to do," I said. "Spraying snow like that."

"Sue me," he said. He looked at my skis sticking out of the snow. "Think I'm scared of someone who doesn't have the guts to do some real surfing?"

He spoke to Cassie. "Are you ready to go rippin'?"

"Sure." Cassie smiled at me. "See you later, Keegan."

The two of them slid away on their snowboards.

The guy really carved the snow. He hit a jump and did a full-spin around.

Cassie had just asked me to trust her.

So why was she snowboarding with a tall guy who was really good on a snowboard? There was one other little thing that bothered me. There was something about this tall snowboarder that made it hard to trust Cassie.

He was wearing a blue knit hat—a hat that could have left fuzzy blue wool behind on the tree near the wire.

chapter six

I watched as they moved down the hill. They didn't move nearly as fast as skiers. Instead they looped up and down the slope.

Maybe I didn't like the guy with the blue hat because Cassie was snowboarding with him. But it seemed to me that he loved showing off. He hit a jump and spun a complete circle in the air. Off the next jump, he spun a circle and a half, landing backward.

"Ooh," I heard someone say, "did you see Sid hit that awesome 5-40?"

Sid? That meant the guy in the blue hat had to be Sid Halloway. His reputation as a snowboarder was the same as mine as a skier. He didn't belong to any team that I knew of, but he was the best snowboarder around.

They were moving farther and farther away, so I started skiing after them.

Sid leaned way back on his snowboard until the nose of it tilted into the air. He grabbed the nose of the snowboard with his hand and rode it like someone doing a wheelie on a bicycle.

A little later he hit another jump and got at least five feet of air. While still in the air, he kicked his heels upward so that the snowboard was almost as high as his waist. He grabbed the board with his hand and, just before landing, let go again.

I hoped he might fall, but he didn't. Instead he did trick after trick. Maybe he knew I was watching him. Maybe he knew I was grumpy about seeing him with Cassie.

They reached the end of the run. I decided to follow, but I didn't want them to see me.

This was the Big Bear ski resort, just outside a small town called Kimberly. I knew all twenty-five runs at the resort. I knew all of the trails through the trees. I should. I have been skiing here since I was eleven years old.

The Pipeline ended where three other ski runs joined together. Then all four runs joined into one big run that led to the main chairlift. I knew I could find them at the bottom. All I had to do was beat them there.

I snapped my boots into my bindings. I grabbed my poles and pushed. Down the hill there was a break in the trees. I turned hard and ducked under some branches. It wasn't much of a trail, but to me skiing was easier than running. I cut in and out of the trees at nearly full speed. A few minutes later, I reached another ski run called the Roller Coaster.

I headed straight downhill in a full run. I passed dozens of slower skiers. At the bottom of the hill the Roller Coaster joined the Pipeline.

I slowed down and moved into some trees at the side of the hill. The trees hid me from anyone coming down the Pipeline.

I waited.

A few minutes later I saw Sid and Cassie. It was easy to find them. Sid had the blue hat and dark blue jacket. Cassie wore the purple ski suit. Both of them were carving major turns in the snow. They hit the bottom and joined the other skiers headed toward the chairlift.

I stayed back. Sid and Cassie didn't notice me. Two things helped me. One, people hardly ever look behind them when they are skiing or snowboarding. Two, there were a lot of skiers on this run. It would have been hard to see me even if Sid or Cassie had looked back.

They surprised me. They didn't stop at the chairlift. They kept on going, right to the ski resort building where people bought lift tickets and ate in the restaurant.

I thought it was strange. Why were they ready to quit so soon? I stayed back and kept watching.

Sid and Cassie stopped at the racks where people leave their skis and snowboards while they go inside. They stepped out of their snowboards and walked into the building.

I skied over to a different set of racks. I kept watching for them. I felt stupid, though. What did I think I was going to learn by following them? I wasn't going to be able to get close enough to listen to what they said. This was my first attempt at being a detective and already I felt like a loser.

Before I could decide what to do next, Sid and Cassie stepped out of the building. They walked back toward their snowboards. I turned my head away. I hoped they did not see my face.

When I looked back, they had picked up their boards.

I thought that was strange too. Why had they gone into the building and then come out again right away? They hadn't even been in long enough to get something to eat.

What they did next was stranger.

They did not go to the chairlift. They walked toward the parking lot with their snowboards. The morning had just started. Were they quitting already? Why?

I stepped out of my skis. When they got around the corner, I ran to the other side of the building. I got to the parking lot just in time to see them put their snowboards into the back of a black van with orange stripes.

Things were getting stranger and stranger. I had seen that van before. It belonged to Budgie McGee.

The van started driving toward me. I stepped back to hide behind the building. It drove past me and out of the parking lot.

I wondered where they were going. I wondered why Budgie was hanging out with a guy who might have been the one to put a wire cable up between two trees. I wondered what Cassie was doing with them.

I couldn't think of one good answer that made sense for any of the questions.

I turned around and went back to grab my skis. Even if I was doing a bad job as a detective, it didn't mean I should waste a good day of skiing.

I set my skis on the snow and stepped into the bindings. I put the ski pole loops around my wrist. I pulled my ski goggles over my eyes.

And I nearly fell backward in surprise.

Sid and Cassie walked around the side of the building. They headed straight toward the ski racks. Budgie must have dropped them off.

Why had they come back?

Sid and Cassie didn't have their snow-boards with them, so what were they doing back at the ski hill?

I kept watching.

They walked right up to the ski racks where they had stopped earlier.

Sid leaned over and pulled a snowboard from the rack. Cassie leaned over and pulled out another snowboard.

It didn't make sense.

Sid slipped his front boot into the snow-board strap. Cassie got ready with her own snowboard.

It still didn't make sense. I had seen them put their snowboards in Budgie's van. I had seen them walk back here without their snowboards. And now they were taking someone else's snowboards.

Both of them pushed off and headed toward the chairlift, just like the hundreds of other people starting out for the day.

Then I knew.

They were on their own snowboards. The first two snowboards they had taken into Budgie's van belonged to someone else. It could only mean one thing.

They had stolen those other two snowboards. And Budgie was now driving away with the stolen snowboards. Weird.

My thoughts went back to the wire that had been stretched across the ski slope. And I began to wonder how much this had to do with that.

The parking lot was jammed, and I could see it was going to take Budgie a while to get to the main road.

I saw a possible solution and made a stupid decision.

chapter seven

The solution was six feet tall, chubby, red-haired and wearing a black ski suit. A bad skier who wanted to be good, whose name was Joe Hardy. Yes, everyone who had ever read one of the *Hardy Boys* mystery books always teased him about it. Me included.

"Chet!" I shouted.

He turned to me, grinning at our inside joke. He looked more like Chet Morton of the Hardy Boys series than Joe Hardy, and I was the only person who ever called him Chet instead of Joe. I stomped toward him in my ski boots.

He was standing beside the ski rack with all his equipment and hadn't yet changed.

"Remember how you've been begging me for lessons?" He was a couple of years older than me, but in our small high school, everybody knew everybody.

"Today?"

"No, but I'll owe you."

"What's the catch?"

"Taxi service," I said. "Right now. Leave your stuff here. We've got to go."

"But I—"

"You just got to the ski hill. I know. I promise I'll make it up to you."

He shrugged. "Why not?"

"Try to keep up," I said. I could see where he'd parked his red Jeep Wrangler. I started to run in my ski boots.

If you've ever tried running in ski boots, you know that it makes you feel like a robot clomping through mud. I snapped the buckles loose and stepped out of them. I held them under my arms, and ran in my sock feet.

My toes were frozen by the time I got to the Jeep.

"Hey," Chet gasped, breathing hard. "What's the deal?"

"Unlock," I said. "Start Jeep. Drive."

He could probably hear my urgency. He hopped in, unlocked the passenger side and started the engine while I leaned in and threw my boots in the back.

I dropped into the passenger seat.

"See the black van with orange stripes?" I said, pointing across him at the other side of the parking lot. "We're going to follow it."

"Like in a movie? Why?"

"If I knew," I said, "we wouldn't have to follow."

Mom's a freak about defensive driving. Or at least about my being a defensive driver when I get finally get my driver's license.

Some kids get lectures about avoiding drugs or cigarettes or alcohol. Not me. I get lectures about the dangers of the road and how every vehicle is a potential killing machine that I need to avoid.

Her main point is very simple. A good driver is not someone who has the skills to get out of trouble. Like being able to bring a sideways skid back under control. No, she always says, a good driver is a driver who can see and avoid trouble long before anything happens. A good driver knows the road is slippery and slows down so that they never have to worry about what to do in a sideways skid.

Another defensive driving trick that my mom drills into me again and again is to make sure there is enough room behind you for the car following you to stop in time.

That's right. Behind you.

Everyone knows that you need to keep space between you and the vehicle in front. If you're going 110 kilometers an hour, for example, keep at least seven car lengths of pavement between your front bumper and the rear bumper of the car ahead. That way, if that car slams on the brakes, you have time to slow down too. And yes, Mom tells me that all the time.

"It's important on icy and snowy roads," mom said about twice a day during the winter, "to slow down and leave room in front of you and behind you. That way if the person behind you can't stop in time, you can ease forward and give them extra room."

Yes, this is a long way of explaining things.

All of this simply means that I'd learned to check the side mirrors a lot to see if trouble was approaching. Because of those repeated lectures, I noticed right away that a middle-aged guy was following us as we left the ski hill.

The guy behind Chet and me was in a late-model car. White. A Ford, I think, but all these new cars look so much the same, his car just blended in with the scenery.

I couldn't see much of his face because he was wearing sunglasses.

But what I did notice was really, really weird.

He had a camera.

He had one hand on the steering wheel and, with his other hand, was taking pictures of Chet's Jeep.

And he kept following us as we followed Budgie's van.

chapter eight

"This isn't as exciting as I thought it might be," Chet said.

Budgie had driven to the nearest gas station and pulled up at a self-serve pump.

"Who said anything about excitement? All I promised you was a ski lesson. Don't pull in, keep driving."

So Chet drove past, with the man in the white Ford still following us.

"How about a U-turn?" I said to Chet.

"That's illegal."

"You wanted excitement. Take it where you can."

"Hah, hah," he said dryly. But made the illegal U-turn anyway. That, at least, made it impossible for the man in the white Ford to stay with us.

Now we were driving back toward the gas station. I thought it would be obvious if we kept circling in the Jeep, so as we neared the gas station, I pointed to the parking lot of a burger place across the street.

"Now you're talking," Chet said, making the turn. "I never say no to food."

"Not today," I said. "Maybe just park behind that truck over there."

"No burgers?"

"Ski lesson number one," I answered as Chet parked behind the truck. "Eat less. Exercise more."

We were hidden from Budgie. I jumped out of the Jeep and peeked around the truck to watch him. He was still pumping gas.

A red Lincoln Navigator pulled up behind Budgie's van, as if the driver was waiting to put gas in too. Except the driver stepped out and, without saying a word, opened the rear door of Budgie's van. Another man got out of the passenger side of the Navigator and stepped to the rear of Budgie's van too.

It didn't look like Budgie had noticed.

The driver was a big man, shaved bald and wearing wraparound sunglasses. His friend was even bigger and had a buzz cut and a goatee. Both of them reached into Budgie's van, pulled out the stolen ski gear and put it into the back of the red Navigator.

I'm not the smartest, but it was obvious to me what was happening. Who would believe me though? It would be my word against theirs.

Unless...

Cell phone!

Goatee Guy handed Budgie an envelope. Budgie opened it and pulled out some money. In an instant, Goatee Guy reached out and grabbed the envelope. He shoved it down the front of Budgie's coat.

I couldn't hear what Goatee Guy was saying. But I could imagine. If that was a payoff for stolen equipment, then Budgie wasn't too smart to pull out the money.

Goatee Guy and his friend moved back to the Navigator. Without a word to Budgie, they drove off.

I jumped back into the Jeep.

"Time to go," I said to Chet. "Another U-turn. Now we're following a Navigator."

"Let me guess," Chet said. "You have no idea why."

"Ski lesson number two: Don't irritate the instructor."

"These lessons don't sound like fun," he said, pulling a quick U-turn.

"Ski lesson number three," I said. "Girls think good skiers are cool."

We caught up to the Navigator.

I took my cell phone out of the inside pocket of my ski jacket. As we got close to the Navigator, I held up my cell phone as if I were making a phone call and used the camera feature to take a photo of the Navigator's license plate.

At the next traffic light, we pulled up beside the Navigator. With my cell phone at my ear, as if I were in conversation with someone, I snapped a photo, hoping I would get a good shot of the passenger.

"Let's head back to the hill," I said.

"That's it?" he said.

"That's it. We'll get together next Monday for a lesson."

He noticed the cell phone in my hand. "Let me give you my cell phone number," he said. "I'm going to watch you put it in your cell and save it. That way you won't have an excuse not to call."

I entered his number and saved it. Then I checked the images on my phone.

Good.

I had a clear shot of the license plate. And not a perfect shot of the passenger, but good enough to make out his features. And a few photos of Goatee Guy handing the envelope to Budgie. Distant shots, but probably good enough.

I didn't know if the photos would be useful, but I knew I had just seen something important.

chapter nine

Chet stopped at the lodge so that I wouldn't have to walk across the parking lot in my ski boots. We set up a time for his ski lesson. Then I jumped out and he drove away.

At the ski hill my skis were where I had left them. For a few minutes I stood in the bright sunshine beside my own skis. The mountainside and the green of the spruce trees were above. Skiers laughed and shouted all around me like they didn't have worries.

But I did.

After a few minutes of standing and doing nothing but thinking, I realized something. Cassie had been the first person down the hill after I had nearly hit the wire. She knew the snowboarder with the blue hat. She had stolen snowboards with him.

If they were such good friends, maybe it wasn't an accident that she showed up after I had fallen. Maybe she was looking to see if the wire had hurt me.

I wanted to smack my head. It didn't make sense. If she knew about the wire, then why did she run into it herself? If she was part of it, she would have known the wire would be there.

I stood in the sunshine a few more minutes.

I thought of something. Two weeks ago, after Garth hit the wire, our coach had found him knocked out. Our coach had not seen the wire himself. Someone must have taken the wire away before he got there. That meant that someone had been waiting beside the wire, ready to untie it, probably with pliers, right after Garth fell.

And if that was true for Garth's accident, then someone must have been waiting beside the wire during my run too. That someone was probably Sid. But because I ducked in time and then went back up the hill, Sid had to jump on his snowboard and get away instead of untying the wire.

All of this would explain Cassie. If she were part of this, she would also think that Sid had pulled down the wire right away. That would explain why the wire surprised her!

I spent a few more minutes in the sunshine thinking about Cassie. I remembered that I had asked Cassie if she was a tourist here on vacation. I remembered that she had not answered my question. I remembered that she had told me her name instead. Did that mean she didn't want me to know why she was at Big Bear?

I thought of the way she spoke, like she was from New York. If she was a tourist, she was probably staying at the resort hotel right here on the slopes.

I had an idea.

I walked toward the front desk of the Big Bear Hotel. My ski boots clunked on the floor. That didn't matter. A lot of people wore their ski boots inside the hotel.

I stopped beneath a stuffed moose head above the front desk. I looked across the desk at a short guy with red hair and lots of freckles.

"Nathan," I said to him with a grin. "Do you remember the day I fixed the bindings on your skis?"

"Sure do," Nathan said. "I still owe you a big favor for that."

"How about now?" I said. "Can you see if someone named Cassie Holt is staying here?"

Nathan frowned. "We're not allowed to give out room numbers to anyone."

"I'm not asking for her room number," I said. "I just want to know if she is staying here."

He kept frowning.

"Nathan," I said, "if someone called the hotel and asked to speak with Cassie Holt, what would you do?"

"I would look her up on the computer and put the call through to her room."

"What if she wasn't staying here?" I asked.

"Then I would tell that person she wasn't at the hotel."

I grinned. "Should I go make that phone call? Or can you tell me right now?"

He grinned back. "I'll look it up."

He typed some letters into his computer keyboard and checked the computer screen.

"Nope," he said. "No Cassie Holt."

"Nuts," I said.

"Hold on," he told me. "There is a John Holt. He has two rooms booked. Do you think one of the rooms is for her?"

"Maybe he is her dad," I said. "Where are they from?"

"Come on, Keegan," he said. "This information is supposed to be private."

I kept grinning. "Remember how you wouldn't have been able to ski with that cute girl all day? But I fixed your bindings right away, didn't I?"

Nathan looked both directions. He leaned forward and whispered. "They are from Long Island, New York. They got here four days ago and they will be checking out a week after Christmas."

He squinted at the screen. "It says they have a Ford Taurus."

Nathan misunderstood my strange look.

"Hey," he said. "We ask for that information in case a car is hit or the lights are on and we need to contact the guest."

"I don't suppose it was white, was it?"

"Yeah," he said. "How did you know?"

"Just a guess," I said. "Thanks. Now I owe you."

Nathan looked at something else on the screen. "This is strange," he whispered.

"What?" I said. "What's strange?"

"It says here that the two rooms have been comped."

"Comped?"

"Yes, comped. It means the rooms are free. So are meals and ski tickets. They don't have to pay a thing for their whole visit here."

"What's strange about that? Doesn't the resort give out free ski weekends all the time?" I asked. "I always hear about them on the radio."

"Usually there is a message on the computer that tells the staff why the room is comped. If it's someone important, we need to know," said Nathan.

"What reason do they give for this one?"

Nathan looked at me. "That's the thing. There is no reason," he said. "And I've never seen something like this before. What do you know about this girl?"

"Not enough," I told Nathan. "Not nearly enough."

chapter ten

I wanted to know more about Cassie Holt.
So I went to the ski shop to rent a snowboard.

"You?" the guy behind the counter asked.
The guy's name was Bubba. He knew me
because sometimes I teach skiing to people
who rent skis from him. He was short and
wide with a beard. "Keegan Bishop? Champion downhill racer? On a snowboard?"

"Sure," I said. "Why not?'

"Are you goofy?"

"Hey," I said. "You don't have to call me names."

He chuckled. "In snowboarding, if you ride with your left foot forward, you're called a regular. If you ride with your right foot forward, you're called a goofy."

"I don't know if I'm goofy or not," I said, feeling goofy just saying it.

"Try this," he said. He put a snowboard on the carpet. "The bindings are set up for a goofy."

I put my feet into the bindings. I imagined myself on a ski hill.

"It feels, um, goofy," I said.

"That's why they call it that," he told me. "Most people are regulars."

He pulled out a different snowboard. "Take the three-day rental, Keegan. It saves you money. The first day will be weird. But don't quit. Once you get used to it, you'll like it." I paid him for three days.

"Yup," he said. "Before you know it, you'll be riding fakie and hitting ollies."

"Huh? Did you just start speaking French or something?"

"You'll be riding backward, jumping bumps and riding the tail of your snowboard."

"Thanks," I said. "Maybe instead of learning how to snowboard, I'll just learn how to talk like a snowboarder."

"Just enjoy the surfing out there," he said.

"I will."

"Oh, by the way," he said as I got ready to leave. "Keep a good eye on your snowboard. It's worth four hundred dollars."

"I won't lose it," I said.

"I'm not worried about you losing it," he told me. "I'm worried about it getting stolen."

"Stolen?"

"Yes," he said. "Stolen. It's been bad this year. From what I'm hearing, every week here at Big Bear thousands of dollars of ski equipment has been stolen."

He whistled. "Add that up. Even if you sold the stolen equipment for half price, that's a lot of money by the end of the season."

I thought of Cassie and Sid walking away with two snowboards. That added up to eight hundred dollars. And it only took them five minutes.

"Boy," I said, "thousands of dollars every week. Isn't it time somebody did something about it?"

I wanted to reach the Pipeline run so that I could see Cassie. I thought she would probably be there with the other snowboarders. I was going to ask her to give me some snowboard lessons. I thought that would be a good way to get to know more about her. And to ask a question or two.

To get to the Pipeline, I first needed to ride the chairlift to the top of the mountain and then take a small run that met up with the Pipeline.

As I got off the chairlift at the top, I fell. It was the first time I had fallen getting off the chairlift since I was eleven years old.

It did not get easier. I fell down so many times that I wished I had bought a butt pad to protect myself.

Little kids on snowboards passed me. Old people on snowboards passed me.

Every time I got up, I wobbled a bit and then fell. At the speed I was going, I wasn't going to reach the Pipeline run until after Christmas.

Then, slowly, I began to catch on. Because I had skied so much already, I knew a little. As I cut across the side of a hill, I learned to dig the uphill edge of my snowboard into the snow to slow down or stop. I learned to turn by skidding one board edge or the other.

I also learned to sink into my turns by bending at the knees and to rise out of my turns by standing again. It helped when I kept my arms level with the slope of the hill.

I decided not to go to the Pipeline right away. Instead I used other runs to practice as I went to the bottom of the mountain.

I moved slowly.

On my skis I could make it all the way down in less than three minutes.

On the snowboard, thirty minutes had passed before I was halfway down. But it was a fun half hour, especially because I didn't go so fast that I was afraid.

I started carving my turns the way I did on skis. I would lean over the inside edge of the snowboard and dig into the snow in a long curve. Then I would shift my weight and curve the other direction by leaning on the other edge of the snowboard.

I was not an expert by the time I reached the bottom of the mountain. Riding a fakie? Nope. I only snowboarded backward by accident. An ollie? No way. My only jumps had happened when I was not able to avoid the big bumps. Wheelies? Nope. I could only dream about getting the nose of my snowboard in the air and riding the back half like a surfboard.

Still, I felt okay. I felt like I wouldn't make a fool of myself by the time I rode the chairlift up again and got on the Pipeline.

And I was right. I didn't make a fool of myself. Sid did it for me.

chapter eleven

I saw Cassie's purple ski suit and blonde hair right away. She was standing with Sid at the top of the Pipeline. He was wearing his blue knitted hat. They were looking down the hill, away from me.

There was a slight wind. It blew uphill in my face as I snowboarded down toward them. I was snowboarding slowly and carefully, so I wasn't making much noise. Also, the wind must have kept them from hearing what little noise I did make.

They were talking. The wind carried their voices right up to me.

"I'm supposed to have dinner with my dad first," Cassie was saying to Sid. "Then I can sneak out of the hotel."

"Just don't forget," he told her. "They want to meet you at nine o'clock."

"Hi guys," I said. I pretended I hadn't heard what they had said. I pointed at the snowboard strapped to my boots. "What do you think?"

"Keegan!" Cassie grinned, like she was happy to see me. "You're on a snow-board!"

"It's kind of fun," I said. "I was hoping you might give me some lessons."

"Sure," she said.

"No," Sid said. "Leave us alone."

"All right," I said, "I lied."

"Huh?" Sid said.

Cassie stared at me. Thoughtfully.

"I didn't stop by because I wanted lessons," I said. "I'm broke."

69

"I'm not a bank," Sid said. "Beat it."

"Broke?" Cassie said.

"Broke," I answered. "I'm willing to do what it takes to not be broke."

"Flip burgers," Sid said. "Go away."

"Come on," I told Sid. "Smart people don't flip burgers."

I paused. I'd given this some thought since leaving the hotel. "Smart people find a way to get envelopes with money."

Cassie kept staring at me. Sid, for a second, said nothing.

"What are you talking about?" he asked when he found his voice.

"Rumors," I said. "That's all."

"You saw Garth in the hospital, didn't you?" Sid was glaring. "What did he say?"

That told me something. Garth was in on this.

"Just rumors," I repeated, wondering what else Sid might spill.

"You noticed Garth's broken legs, didn't you?" Sid said. "You don't want to mess with…"

He snapped his mouth shut.

With a couple of guys in a Lincoln Navigator? I didn't say this out loud, though. The less Sid knew about what I knew, the better.

"I don't understand," I said instead. "Garth told me it was an accident."

"It was," Sid said. "Just be careful accidents don't happen to you."

"I ski fast," I said, "but I'm careful."

Sid gave me a nasty grin. "But in case you haven't noticed, right now—you're not on skis."

Before I could answer, he pushed me. I went sliding down the hill, almost at full speed. And directly below me was a little girl on skis!

The girl was skiing very slowly. Her little legs were wide apart as she did her best not to fall. She was wearing a cute yellow hat and she was hardly higher than my knees. If I hit her, I thought, I could break every bone in her body.

If I had been on skis, I could have missed her easily.

But I was on a snowboard. I didn't think I could turn in time. I was afraid if I tried to turn too quickly, the snowboard would slide out from under me. If that happened, I would slide into her feet first. The snowboard would wipe her out.

I was shooting straight toward her. I couldn't fall. I couldn't turn. I felt like a rocket aimed directly at her back. For a horrible heartbeat, I got a picture in my head of my brother stuck on the tracks and a train roaring in behind him.

No, I told myself. I was so angry I didn't have time to be scared. I concentrated on my every move to time this just right.

I aimed the tip of my snowboard right between her skis.

I brought my hands down and grabbed her waist. Instead of crashing into her back, I lifted her and her skis off the ground.

It worked. She was in my arms and traveling at my speed. Her skis were on different sides of my waist.

"Wheeeee!" she screamed. "Daddy, this is so fun!"

It wasn't fun for me. I still had to come to a stop. Slowly, very slowly, I turned my snowboard and dug the hillside edge into the snow. Slowly, very slowly, we began to slow down.

"Wheeee!" she said again. "I like this Daddy!"

When we were finally stopped, I set her down. She turned around and looked at me. Her little jaw dropped in surprise.

"You're not my daddy!" she screamed. She began to cry.

Sid and Cassie snowboarded up to us.

Cassie put her arms around the little girl's shoulders. "We'll find your daddy," Cassie said.

The girl stopped crying. A man higher up on the hill shouted down to us.

"See," Cassie told her, "your daddy is coming right now."

I moved away from Cassie and the little girl. I hoped that when her dad reached her, he would pick up his daughter first. This way he wouldn't be able to go after me.

Sid followed me. "Don't think you're

a hero. If you don't stop hanging around, you're going to get hurt. Real bad."

"Oh yeah?" I said. It was all I could think of saying. I was no hero. If he only knew the truth.

"Yeah," he said. "Go ask Budgie. Of course, you'll have to visit him in the hospital."

"Budgie?" I said. "He's hurt too?"

Sid smiled. "Didn't you hear? He got his van into a little accident an hour ago. That's what happens to people who mess with us."

chapter twelve

Instead of going home that afternoon, I let my parents know I would be staying at the Big Bear ski hill. That's the way I do things. It saves them from worrying. Ever since the day that my little brother Evan died, they've worried about getting another phone call from the police with terrible news.

I get rooms at the staff rate because I sometimes work as a ski instructor. I stay at the resort when I want to get an early start on the slopes, so my parents weren't at all surprised when I told them I wasn't going to be home.

When I got hungry, I ate a few greasy burgers. When I got bored, I read some ski magazines.

I did what I needed to do to kill time. Cassie was supposed to be meeting somebody. If I could find out who, maybe then I would know why. Why had Garth and Budgie been hurt? Why was Cassie in on this? Was she in danger too? Why was this all happening?

I planned to follow Cassie when she left the Big Bear hotel. I hung out in the hotel lobby because I wanted to stay warm for as long as possible. At night the mountain air is very cold.

At quarter to nine I went outside and stepped into the shadows of some trees. From there I could watch the doors of the hotel without being seen.

Just before nine o'clock Cassie hurried out of the hotel. She was easy to follow because she didn't look behind her, and I was able to stay in trees most of the way.

She surprised me. She went straight toward the chairlift on the side of the mountain.

I kept following.

The chairlift was quiet. It was easy to see, though. There was a bright moon, and the light bounced off the snow. The trees and the chairlift were dark. The snow was gray. It seemed like I was walking through a black-and-white movie.

Two guys were waiting for her at the chairlift. I saw that they were on skis.

Skiing? At night? What was happening?

There were lots of trees at the bottom of the hill, so I was able to get closer without being seen. What I saw, though, I didn't like.

One of the men pulled out a knit scarf and wrapped it around her throat!

"What is going on?" she said, her voice strangled. Her voice reached me clearly across the cold mountain air.

"What is going on?" the man said. It wasn't Sid. I had never heard his voice before. "You're going for a little ride."

For a moment his face was turned enough to catch some light. It was the bald guy who had been driving the red Lincoln Navigator. The other guy stepped out of his skis. He picked up something that had been leaning against a tree. I saw a goatee in the shadows of his face. The passenger from the Navigator!

"Hold this snowboard," he told her.

While the bald guy held her in place with the scarf as a noose, Goatee Guy went to the chairlift building. He smashed a side window, reached in and unlocked the door. He stepped inside. A little later the giant motors started. The chairs on the chairlift began to move.

Goatee Guy stepped outside again. He got in his skis. He sidestepped close to Cassie.

The motors of the chairlift hummed loudly. I could not hear what he said.

I saw him point at the chairlift.

The three of them moved toward a chair. They got on. The chair took them—Cassie, a snowboard and two men wearing skis—up the mountain.

What could I do?

By the time I got the police, or any other help, it might be too late. There had been another time when I had let fear stop me from doing what was right. And then it had been too late. Much too late.

I wasn't going to let anything like that happen again. I waited until they were part-way up the mountain. Then I ran toward the chairlift. I got on one of the chairs.

I was afraid if they looked back they would see me, so I laid down across the chair. I hoped I would be lost in the shadows.

The chairlift carried me up the mountain behind them.

Though I was in the shadows of the chair, I was able to see them in the moonlight. They were at least twelve chairs ahead. The ski lift took us higher and higher.

I knew this was crazy.

What could I do against these two large men when they had Cassie and could snap her neck in a second?

I quickly realized that it would have been much smarter to have gone for help. If they were going to kill her, they would have done it right away. I could have found someone to help in less than five minutes. But because I had stupidly decided to be a hero, nobody knew what was happening. And I had no way of getting off the chair until it reached the top of the hill. Now if something went wrong, instead of just Cassie being in trouble, it would be both of us. And no one would rescue us.

I was so scared I felt the familiar feeling in my stomach that told me I might throw up. I was no hero.

I knew why I had jumped onto the chairlift. Once, years before, I had looked up at a train coming from out of nowhere and I had let myself be frozen with fear. I had waited too long to help someone who needed me. I didn't need to hate myself more by running away again.

Besides, it was too late to change my mind. The only way to get off this chairlift was to wait until it reached the top.

I began to worry about something else. The two men had skis. Cassie had the snowboard they had given her. How could I keep up? Walking through mountain snow is not easy. If the snow is not packed from skis, you sink up to your waist—or deeper.

Then I remembered. At the top of the chairlift, there is a ski patrol sled. It is kept there for emergencies. If someone gets hurt, a member of the ski patrol uses the sled to carry the injured person down the hill.

Could I use the sled to follow these three?

I decided I could. I would lie on it and drag my feet to steer it. As long as I stayed far enough behind them, it would work.

I sure hoped so because a few minutes later, we reached the top of the mountain.

My planning went to waste. When I got off the chair, the man with the goatee was waiting for me.

chapter thirteen

"You think we couldn't see you on the chair-lift, kid?" Goatee Guy asked. "Now tell us. What are you doing?"

I looked at the bald man who was holding Cassie with the scarf around her neck like a noose.

"Are you all right?" I asked Cassie.

"I get it," the bald man said. "Puppy love."

"Let him go," Cassie said. "Keegan doesn't know anything about this."

"Keegan?" the man said. "Keegan Bishop? The racer?"

He laughed. "Two for the price of one. Now the girl's old man won't dare try anything."

"My dad?" Cassie said.

"Your dad. Mister Cameraman. We saw you with him today, same guy who had been following us. Took his license number. Bribed a kid at the rental agency to give us his name. Googled it and discovered he was a detective. New York, right? Didn't take long to figure out that you were trying something."

"Yup," Goatee Guy said. "Figured we'd get you up here alone. Find out exactly why you wanted to meet. Are you wired?"

"I don't know what you are talking about," Cassie said.

"You're a bad liar. We can search you here and now. Or you can just give it up."

After several seconds Cassie sighed. "Pocket of my jacket. Voice-activated tape recorder."

The bald guy patted for it, found it and removed the cassette.

"It's not going to help," Cassie said. "Kid-napping us is just going to make it worse."

"Oh? Because your dad has photos?"

Her silence confirmed it.

"Tell your daddy," Goatee Guy said, "that this is the digital age. He needs to upgrade his equipment."

"I...I don't understand," Cassie said.

"If he used a digital camera, we wouldn't be up here. But he's still using a camera that takes film. Which we now have."

"What!"

"Not tough to break into a hotel room," the guy said. "We've got everything. And now we've got you."

The scarf was still around her neck. I needed to keep the conversation going for as long as possible. Maybe someone had seen us go up. Maybe security had spotted the broken window in the chairlift building. The longer we kept talking, the better the chance we might get help.

"Garth and Budgie were stealing skis," I said. "They always made sure they were taking equipment that looked like their own. If they got caught, all they had to do was pretend they grabbed the wrong equipment."

Goatee Guy snorted. "Another detective. Think you'll get off the hill before we're long gone?"

"I'm right though."

"Big deal."

"As long as they always took skis that looked like theirs," I said, "nothing could go wrong. How much were they making?"

"Couple hundred bucks a day," Goatee Guy answered. "Just for walking into the parking lot with the wrong equipment."

"So why are Garth and Budgie in the hospital?" I asked.

"Simple. They got greedy. The way it works, they steal the equipment. They give it to us. We find buyers. We give them half of what we make. But Garth and Budgie wanted to go into business on their own. We don't like that. Our snowboarding buddy set up a cable for Garth to hit. Today we did a little trick with the tires on Budgie's van. They both learned their lessons."

"There's one thing I don't understand," I said. At least we were talking, not getting beat up. "Why did Sid set up a cable between the trees for me? I'm not part of this."

"Budgie switched jersey numbers with you, remember?" Goatee Guy answered. "All you racers look the same with your helmets on. I was watching the starting gate with binoculars. When I saw Budgie's number, I called Sid. He was waiting to set the wire. It was going to work the same way it did with Garth. As soon as Budgie hit the wire, Sid would take it down again and leave on his snowboard. Of course, you were wearing Budgie's number. So we had to wait to get Budgie."

The bald guy finally spoke. "Hey! We don't have all night."

"What are you going to do?" I asked.

"Cassie is going to have a snowboarding accident," the bald guy said. "We'll break her leg and leave her on the mountain. We ski out. She stays behind. Then we call her old man and tell him to start looking. That will distract him and everyone else long enough for us to be hundreds of miles away by the time she's found."

Goatee Guy said, "What should we do with Joe Detective here?"

"Nothing," I said, "especially if Cassie throws me the snowboard."

"Huh?" Goatee Guy said.

"Unless you want to spend all night trying to walk up and over the other side of the mountain," I said, "the only way off the hill is straight down. And I am going to get down before you do and call the cops. So you'd be stupid to do anything to Cassie. I'm not going to stand back and take the chance that someone else might die. Not again."

"What do you mean, not again?" Cassie said. "Have—"

"The snowboard, Cassie," I said. "Now!"

The guy holding her by the scarf tried to yank her back, but it was too late.

She tossed the snowboard just ahead of me. It landed and started sliding downhill away from me.

I dove onto it. Belly first. The bindings hit my stomach hard. But I didn't care. I was on my way down the hill.

I spun the snowboard to the right. It tilted and nearly threw me into the snow.

The hill was so steep I was already at full speed.

If I didn't slow down, the snowboard would kill me instead of them doing it.

I remembered what I had planned to do with the sled. I dug my toes into the ground.

It slowed me some and brought me to a stop. But I didn't have much time.

Goatee Guy behind me was on skis!

I looked back.

He was a dark shadow against the moonlight and snow. And he was already moving toward me.

I stood as fast as I could. I stepped into the bindings on the snowboard. I strapped them tight around my shoes. I started down the hill.

He was on skis. I was on a snowboard. And I was in for the run of my life!

chapter fourteen

I knew if I fell, I was dead. He would catch me before I could get to my feet again.

I had to cover over a kilometer of ski run before I reached the resort buildings. He was faster on skis than I was on my snowboard. I had only learned how to snowboard that afternoon.

The good news was that he would have to go slower in the moonlight than in daylight.

I would not have to worry as much. I knew nearly ever bump and dip on this ski hill.

The other good news was that Cassie was safe, for now. They didn't dare do anything to her, because if I got away, they'd be caught. But I would have to make it to the bottom without killing myself by wrapping my body around a tree.

I turned hard into a corner.

Ahead of me the ski hill broke into two runs. One was called the Hammer, because it hit you hard with moguls. I didn't want to hit moguls. They are like tiny hills. You have to ski around them. Not through them or over them. I can handle moguls at high speeds on skis. But not on a snowboard.

I took the other run. The Monster. It was steep, but smoother than the Hammer. I picked a straight line and crouched.

The wind tore at my hair and face.

I caught a small bump. I was going so fast it threw me into the air. I concentrated on keeping my knees bent. I concentrated on keeping the snowboard pointed down the hill.

Whomp!

I landed hard and tilted to one side. My hand banged the ground. I pushed off and kept on my feet.

I didn't dare look back to see if he was close.

Was I scared?

So scared I could hardly think. And I still had a half kilometer to go.

I cut to one side, then the other. I made sure I zigged and zagged so that he couldn't guess where I was going.

As I made a turn I saw him over my shoulder. He was close. So close there wasn't room to park a bus between us.

I knew I didn't have enough room to outrun him.

I did know there was a trail through the trees that came out near the hotel parking lot.

I cut hard. I almost skidded and wiped out.

The black outlines of the trees were coming at me fast. I turned a bit more and hit the trail through the trees.

If I fell now, I didn't need to worry about getting caught. Slamming into the trees on either side of the trail would do more damage than a dozen big bald guys.

I ducked. I bobbed. I fought to keep my balance on the snowboard. Somehow I managed to stay upright. Then I shot through a gap in the trees out into the open of another run.

I was nearly at the bottom of the hill.

Then I hit another bump.

Because I was standing nearly straight up, and because my arms were too high in the air, I lost my balance.

The snowboard flipped me high in the air. I did a half turn. My feet were higher than my head. Coming down felt like slow motion.

I tried to get my hands out to block my fall. It didn't work.

My head banged into the hard packed snow. I tumbled hard. And lost my snowboard as it whizzed forward and smashed into the trees ahead.

As I finished rolling, the bottom of my left leg hit a tree. The pain was like a white-hot knife, and I knew my ankle was broken.

But it could have been worse. It could have been my skull.

I looked up, expecting Goatee Guy to be all over me.

It took me a couple of seconds to realize Goatee Guy had been so close behind me that he hadn't been able to stop until he was a hundred meters below me.

But by the way he was looking back up the hill, he knew exactly where I was.

Which was too far away from the bottom of the hill to have any chance to get away.

I tried to get up. I nearly screamed at the pain of my left ankle.

There was no way I could try to run. I was like a mouse with its leg pinned in a trap.

Goatee Guy began to push his way back up the hill. Slowly he got closer and closer, stepping into the side of the hill with his skis.

What could I do?

My cell phone!

I pulled off my gloves and reached inside my jacket and found it.

At best, I had a couple of minutes.

I flipped it open, grateful that the back-light allowed me to see the keypad.

As my fingers grew cold, I began hitting the numbers.

Then a thought hit me.

What if Goatee Guy found the cell phone on me and took it? But I couldn't throw it away. Not in this deep snow. It was too valuable. Unless I could find a way to make sure I didn't need it.

Instead of calling the hotel for security, I decided to do something else.

And when Goatee Guy finally reached me, I was sitting and trying to pretend that I wasn't sweating with pain.

He was puffing hard. "You're going to pay for this."

He dug into his pocket. And pulled out a cell phone. He punched a button. "Yeah," he said, "I've got him. Break the girl's leg and leave her up there. And trust me, when I finish with him, he won't be going anywhere either."

"No!" I said. I held up my own cell phone. I'd kept it hidden behind my back. "I had enough time to call for help. See?"

I pointed. At the bottom of the hill we could see pinpricks of light. Flashlights. People rushing toward the chairlift.

He cursed.

"Hey," he said into his own cell. "Don't hurt the girl. We've got to run. Meet you at the bottom of the other chairlift."

A pause. Then Goatee Guy nodded. "Yeah, I'll take his cell phone. That way it will take longer for them to find him."

Another pause. "You're right. But I can take care of that."

He snapped his phone shut.

"You didn't change anything, you know. We'll still get away as planned." He snorted. "Of course I'll need to make sure you keep your mouth shut. First, give me the phone."

I threw it into the snow as far as I could.

"No big deal," he said. "Doesn't look like you're able to go anywhere anyway."

He took off one of his skis and balanced on the other ski above me. I couldn't go anywhere. Not with the broken ankle.

He lifted the ski high above my head.

"Your choice," he said. "Close your eyes, or watch it coming. Either way, I'm going to make sure you won't be yelling for help."

I wanted to have the courage to keep my eyes open. But, as usual, I was a coward. I shut my eyes and covered my head as best I could.

But it didn't help.

Everything, as they say, went black. Very very black.

chapter fifteen

It was the nightmare that smothered me in a dark pit. I was on my bicycle, looking up the road behind me. I yelled at my brother for how stupid he was to get his bike stuck in the train tracks. Just like the last time I had this nightmare, and the time before that, the locomotive rounded the corner, with a big white headlight that was painful to look into even in daylight. I yelled at my brother to jump off his bike.

My brother's pants were caught in his bicycle chain—the bicycle that was stuck in the railroad tracks. He needed help. I was too scared to move and by the time I did, it was too late.

The next thing I knew we were all at the hospital—my parents, my brother and me. The doctors and nurses said they were so sorry but they couldn't do a thing. I lied and told my parents I couldn't have done anything either...

I woke up on a couch in the lobby of the Big Bear Hotel.

The first thing I saw was the stuffed moose head above the front desk. I had seen it many times before. This was the first time I felt sorry for it. My head felt as if someone had cut it off my body and stuffed it too.

"Are you all right, son?" a man asked. He stood above me.

I blinked my eyes. I did not know him.

"My parents," I said. "Someone call them and tell them I'm okay."

"I'll do it," he said. He smiled. "I'm John Holt, Cassie's father."

I tried to sit up. "She's...on...the...mountain!"

It hurt to talk. But I had to tell him. "They...want...to...break...her...leg!"

"Relax, son," he said. "She's right here."

He stepped away and Cassie stepped up to the couch. Still in her purple ski suit. Still as beautiful as I remembered.

Behind her were policemen and other people. They were talking to each other and were not looking at us. John Holt went over to them. That left Cassie and me alone.

"I hope you're all right," she said. "The doctors said it was a mild concussion. They couldn't find any broken bones."

I would hate to know what a serious concussion felt like.

"I'm okay," I said. I managed to sit up. "Glad you are too."

"Didn't take the security guys long to find me once they got to the top," she said. "You took a little longer."

Cassie smiled. I liked her smile. I thought it would be good to get her to smile as much as I could.

"Your dad's a detective," I said. "You weren't part of this."

She nodded. "Dad was hired by the Big Bear ski resort. He used to be a cop for the New York City Police. He retired and became a private detective."

"And the Big Bear ski resort hired him and comped your rooms."

"The manager knew it was really strange how much equipment was stolen every week. He knew it couldn't be people who just took the snowboards and skis to use themselves. Too much was being taken for that. He thought it might be something more. He even thought it might be Sid and Garth and Budgie. But the manager wanted to know who they were stealing the equipment for."

She sat. Close. I liked that.

"I was trying to help my dad," she said. "He didn't know it, but I decided to make friends with Sid and Budgie. That's why I was following you down the hill the first time we met. I thought you were Budgie because you were wearing his number."

"That makes sense," I said. "Only you didn't know about the wire."

"No," she said. "I didn't know that they were trying to get Budgie like they got Garth. And then I left when you called me a detective because I thought maybe you were involved too."

"Is that why your dad followed me this morning?"

"Yes," she said. "I told him you might be part of it."

"The meeting tonight?" I asked.

"Dad knew about that. When I told him I had found a way to meet the guys who bought the stolen equipment, Dad was angry that I had put myself in danger. He finally let me go to the meeting, but only because he was going to follow and arrest the guys. All I needed to do was talk to them."

"The voice-activated tape recorder."

"All I needed was for them to say enough to prove their guilt. Except, of course, that didn't work. Still, I'm glad my dad was close by to help bring me down the hill after you made your call."

She frowned. "Even if the cops find them, we've got no proof. They destroyed my dad's camera. All his film."

"Maybe not," I said.

"Trust me," she said. "It's all gone."

"I mean maybe you do have proof." I told her about my cell phone photos.

"Wow!" She clapped. "Where's your cell phone?"

"I had to throw it into the snow," I said.

"But the snow's at least ten feet deep in those trees. We might not find it until the snow melts. And by then the phone won't work."

"Probably not," I said. "That's why I sent a text message to a guy named Joe Hardy and attached the photos."

"You can't be serious."

"That's his name: Joe Hardy. Everyone teases him about it, but—"

"I don't care about his name. He really has the photos?"

I gave a big grin. "Case solved, ma'am."

She leaned forward and kissed my check. "You are a sweetheart!"

I wanted to agree, but I couldn't. Not with the black secret that drove me to prove, on every ski run, that I wouldn't lose to fear again.

She frowned. "You've been asking me a lot of questions, but I have one for you. What did you mean when you said you wouldn't take the chance that someone else might die?"

I thought of what I should tell her. I had to talk to someone someday, or bust, or turn into a rock. But if I told her, she wouldn't like me.

"Look," I said. "What if there was a person who was once so scared as a kid that he didn't do something in time to save another kid? And what if that person had never told his mom or dad what had really happened?"

She didn't answer right away, as if she knew how important my question was.

"I think that person's parents would realize kids aren't superheroes," she finally said. "Even most grown-ups would be too scared to do the right thing. So it would be unfair for that person to blame himself. And it would be good for that person to tell his parents."

"Yeah," I said, like it wasn't a big deal one way or another. But, of course, it was. And I'd think about what she said.

It was awkward for a few moments. I coughed.

"Well," she said, "my dad and I still have nearly ten days of vacation left."

"I hope you enjoy it," I said. Since I wouldn't be able to ski with a broken ankle, I didn't have a chance of seeing her on the slopes.

"You dummy," she said. "Can't you get anything right?"

"Huh?"

"I just told you I have ten days left. That's when you're supposed to ask if someone like me could spend some time with someone like you."

She smiled and gave me another kiss on the cheek. "Ten days can be a lot of time, don't you think?"